MW01596195

Table of Contents

What Exactly is Whole30?

One year out the door and another step right in. It's January, the perfect time for New Year's resolutions, such as "this time, I'll definitely lose weight!" Well, that's both easier and harder than it sounds. Losing body weight is very easy, all you have to do is drink a diuretic, such as black tea, to flush out the excess water and voilà –a couple pounds are gone. Though, they're going to come right back when you rehydrate and stop the diuretic. Losing body fat, now that's an achievement.

The thing is, the body clings on to body fat as if though its life depended on it because that's actually the case. Every bit of unspent energy you eat turns to fat and goes to fat cells that inflate like balloons, stretching way beyond their original size and it's not coming out unless it's absolutely necessary. As far as the body's internal calculator is concerned, more fat means more energy and longer survival if food becomes scarce, love handles are damned. The fact that modern industrial food is designed to be instantly digested doesn't help because it's making you constantly crave for more. But, there's one way out, a mysterious mentorclad in a black robe that approaches you and whispers, "I hear you need my assistance" and you bow your head, "Diet Sensei, it has come to this."

To be clear, any kind of planned feeding can be called a diet, so don't fret about talking, reading or trying a diet. Eating only bananas is a diet; fasting and drinking only water is a diet; eating only homemade ice cream is a diet, and so is the Whole30. The trick is to try all sorts of diets and find one that works for you and that you can maintain for the rest of your life with little effort. In essence, Whole30 asks you to follow a specific feeding plan for 30 days to clean up your body from the inside, even if just a little bit.

What Are the Rules of Whole 30?

Let's be clear: nobody is going to check up on you and there are no penalties for not following the rules. This is more what you'd call "guidelines" than actual rules. In fact, it's perfectly normal for a fresh dieter to feel a craving for sugary treats and succumb at any given time. That's exactly why they're such a danger, since sugar raises the insulin levels, signaling the body to convert energy into fat and store it. So, if you can estimate how much sugar you're ingesting every day, you've achieved tremendous progress in the Whole30 diet.

There are all sorts of sugars (also known as carbohydrates or carbs) and each of them impacts the body in a slightly different way. In nature, carbs are found in pretty much everything that's edible, including insects and leaves, which is how animals can eat them and survive. For humans, the most common sources of carbs are grains and fruits, but an important thing to note is that carbs in these natural sources always come with a truckload of nutrients that make you feel satiated when you eat them. Once the food industry figured out distilled carbs actually cause addiction and make you feel hungrier, they suddenly found their place in all the isles of the supermarket.

So, the challenge is to learn how to recognize these distilled carbs and stay away from them for 30 days. Whole30 asks you to skip: alcohol, dairy, table sugar, grains, and legumes. Yes, this includes bread. At every step of the way, you should listen to your body and notice how it's reacting to presence or absence of certain foods. Over time, you'll learn that you have a certain subconscious program that makes you eat the way you do. The genius idea of Whole30 is that it exposes the program and lets you hack it the way you want to.

What Can You Eat On the Whole30?

Protein, carbs, and fats are three major ways we get calories so the body can keep working. Since we'll be dropping processed carbs, this leaves protein, natural carbs, and fats. So, not only are you not losing out on the variety, you'll finally find out how many interesting and healthy foods there are out there, waiting to be discovered and tasted.

You can get protein from poultry and fish, the two healthiest meat groups. Though poultry is readily available, it also has the blandest taste imaginable. You know the phrase "tastes like chicken"? It's what we say whenever we eat something nondescript. So, your job is to find all sorts of spices and make your plate a carnival of colors and textures. Red meat works too, though be careful not to overdose on salt, which causes the body to retain water to flush it out, raising the blood pressure and burdening the kidneys. 3g (half a teaspoon) of salt is quite enough each day, but if you can lower it by any amount, your heart will jump for joy.

PROTEIN
Chicken
Turkey
Minced Beef/Lamb/Pork
Sausages (grain & sugar free)
Bacon (sugar & nitrate free)
Cooked Ham (sugar free)
Lamb/Pork/Beef Joint
Salmon
Cod
Haddock
Smoked Salmon
Prawns
Eggs

FRUIT
Apples	Melon
Bananas	Oranges
Blackberries	Peaches
Blueberries	Pears
Cherries	Pineapple
Dates	Plums
Grapefruit	Raspberries
Grapes	Strawberries
Kiwi	
Lemons	
Limes	
Mango	

OILS
Olive Oil
Extra Virgin Olive Oil
Coconut Oil
Clarified Butter

VEGETABLES
Aubergine	Kale
Avocado	Lettuce
Asparagus	Mushrooms
Beetroot	Onions
Broccoli	Parsnips
Butternut Squash	Peppers
Cabbage	Potatoes
Carrots	Spinach
Cauliflower	Sweet Potato
Celery	Tomatoes
Courgette	Turnips
Cucumber	
Garlic	
Green Beans	

STORE CUPBOARD
Cashew Nuts
Hazelnuts
Macadamia Nuts
Nut Butter (not peanut)
Dessicated Coconut
Coconut / Almond Flour
Cocoa Powder

Coconut Milk
Almond Milk
Coconut Water

Curry Paste
Chilli Sauce
Tinned Tomatoes / Passata
Olives
Red & White Wine Vinegar
Stock
Herbs & Spices

Natural carbs are found in fruits, so grab an apple, orange, mango, pineapple and a banana, chop them all up in a bowl and squeeze some lemon juice on top for a delicious fruit salad that never goes out of style. Now, if you try eating nothing but fruit for any length of time you'll notice how it doesn't really make you hungry for more like candy does. This is because fruit generally has dietary fiber that makes you chew through it and expands in the stomach, causing you to feel full and cleaning your gut. 20g of dietary fiber a day is it all it takes to make your digestion work like a Swiss watch.

Finally, fats are found in meat, some veggies, and vegetable oils. There are several types of fats and the jury is still out on what kind is the best, but the easiest solution is to have a healthy variety of different kinds. So, one day fish, another bacon, then avocado and so on. Since fats tend to fill you up, there's no need to mind how much you're eating but beware of sour cream and full-fat dairy since the calories can add up fast.

What You Can't Eat

The idea behind Whole30 is to steadily reduce the things we overdose on, but you shouldn't obsess over it. At first, just keep track of how much of alcohol, dairy, table sugar, grains and legumes you're taking until you've created sort of a counter in your head that automatically warns you when you've done too much. You don't have to be perfectly exact, an estimate will do at first. When you get this nagging voice that tells you to quit it, you're ready for Whole30.

Eventually, you'll get the urge to simply binge on your favorite and that's perfectly understandable as well. Even then it's not a problem if you decide to make that a planned reward for something you've done. So, finished that big project and you've been eyeing that chocolate bar? You've deserved it and it will make you work even harder with the next project knowing there's a sweet reward.

THE RULES
No added sugar, real or artificial
No alcohol
No grains
No legumes
No dairy
No carrageenan, MSG or sulfites
No baked goods, junk foods or
treats with approved ingredients

The point of dieting isn't to torture yourself but to make a comfortable way of living that is in line with health recommendations and that suits you. In the end, it's not that any of these foods are bad on their own, it's just that we're using too much of them without even realizing how much damage we're causing to our own bodies in the long run.

Benefits of Whole30

A diet rich in refined carbs tends to raise the insulin levels, causing obesity. When there's too much body fat, it becomes a genuine internal organ, releasing over 50 inflammatory factors and its own hormones that ruin your health. Worse yet, obesity means the knees and other joints in the body have to endure a lot of added pressure at all times, which makes them wear out much faster. All of this is because of added calories, so any little bit of it you can take out of your diet will set you on the right path to having a lean, healthy body.

Drinking too much alcohol puts great stress on the liver that tends to regenerate fast, but even it has limits. When the person is also obese, the body uses the liver as an extra storage unit, weighing it down even further and making it work slower to process the alcohol out of the body. Again, limiting alcohol consumption while lowering insulin levels and calories ingested makes the body start spending the fat reserves and helps the liver recuperate.

Finally, legumes tend to ferment in the bowels, feeding harmful bacteria and causing gas buildup. If you can control your legume intake, you'll reduce bloating and avoid gut bacteria overgrowth.

Why 30 Days?

Once you get on a diet, you'll spend years searching for just the right variety. Eventually, you'll be dieting for a lifetime but a newbie dieter needs to have an easy, sexy and approachable number so 30 it is. On a serious note, 30 days is a typical month and makes you feel like you've achieved something amazing. That counts too and when you start dieting, you'll find it difficult to ignore your favorite comfort foods without there being a real sense of progress.

Why It's Not A Typical Diet?

A typical diet is much stricter than Whole30, usually promising results and relying on your strict adherence to the rules. Whole30 isn't like that because it lets you pick and choose the best way to plan, start and end it. Whole30 can be scaled up or down and adjusted to your needs in stride.

What is Instant Pot?

Instant Pot is your magical little helper in the kitchen that merrily cooks things in a fraction of the time it usually takes. With it, you'll find yourself hard pressed to go back to regular pots and pans.

A team of Canadian experts led by Dr. Robert Wang set out in 2009 to make cooking a dream come true. They formed the Instant Pot Company and started producing a whole line of cookware to help every industrious person become the alpha cook. Using an instant pot is a foolproof ordeal: pour some liquid in (water, stock), add the food ingredients in, season, close and let it run. The jolly instant pot will do everything automatically and you just have to savor the delight.

Is it healthy to cook in a pressure cooker?

Pressure cookers have been around for several centuries and they're perfectly healthy since they use only steam and heat. By the way, the steam makes heat go straight to the core of a food item, cooking it in no time.

There is an instant pot for every purpose, and your job is to try as many as you can and reach that conclusion on your own. In short, the one that you fall in love with after trying is the right one.

Cooking Times

Total Time: 1 hour and 20 minutes

Nutrition Facts

Serving size: 1/12 of a recipe (3 ounces)

Percent daily values based on the Reference Daily Intake (RDI) for a 2000 calorie diet.

Nutrition information calculated from recipe ingredients.

Amount Per Serving

Calories 203,01

Calories From Fat (66%) 132,99

% Daily Value

Total Fat 15,8g 24%

Saturated Fat 1,71g 9%

Cholesterol 46,5mg 16%

BREAKFAST

Almond, Banana and Carrot Bread (Instant Pot)

Ingredients

2 Tbsp Extra-virgin olive oil

3 eggs

3 ripe bananas

1/2 cup stevia sweetener

2 tsp vanilla extract

1 1/2 cup almond flour or ground almonds

1/2 tsp sea salt

1/2 tsp baking soda

1/4 tsp ground cinnamon

1/2 cup almonds, chopped

3/4 cup grated carrots

2 cups water for Instant Pot

Instructions

1. Grease the loaf pan with olive oil; set aside.
2. Whisk together the eggs, banana, stevia, olive oil, and vanilla extract.
3. In a separate bowl, combine the almond flour, salt, baking soda, and ground cinnamon.
4. Combine the egg mixture to the flour mixture and stir well. A
5. Add the almonds and carrots; stir well.
6. Pour the batter into prepared loaf pan.
7. Put a steamer rack in the Instant Pot with 2 cups of water in the liner.
8. Place the loaf pan on trivet.
9. Lock lid into place and set on the MANUAL setting for 30 minutes.
10. When the timer beeps, press "Cancel" and naturally release pressure for 15 minutes and quick release remaining pressure.
11. Let cool, slice and serve.

Breakfast Vegetable Omelet (Instant Pot)

Ingredients

1 Tbsp lard

2 scallions, finely sliced

1 bell pepper, cut into thin strips

2 zucchini sliced

6 eggs

Instructions

1. Press SAUTÉ button on your Instant Pot and heat the lard.
2. Sauté the scallions for about 3-4 minutes.
3. Add the chopped peppers and cook for about 2 minutes. Add the zucchini and sauté for another 2- 3 minutes.

4. Whisk the eggs in a bowl. Add salt and pepper to taste. Pour the eggs mixture over the vegetables in your Instant Pot.
5. Lock lid into place and set on the MANUAL setting for 5 minutes.

Servings: 12

Cooking Times

Total Time: 35 minutes

Coconut Muffins (Instant Pot)

Nutrition Facts

Serving size: 1/12 of a recipe (2,8 ounces).

Percent daily values based on the Reference Daily Intake (RDI) for a 2000 calorie diet.

Nutrition information calculated from recipe ingredients.

Amount Per Serving

Calories 191,66

Calories From Fat (70%) 134,32

% Daily Value

Total Fat 15,65g 24%

Saturated Fat 9,25g 46%

Cholesterol 93mg 31%

Ingredients

1 cup coconut flour

1 cup almond flour

1 tsp baking soda

1 tsp of sea salt

1 cup almonds and macadamia nuts, finely chopped

6 large, free-range eggs

4 Tbsp stevia sweetener or to taste

1 cup almond milk (unsweetened)

1 cup coconut oil, melted

1 cup cacao chips

Instructions

1. Line12 muffin tins with parchment paper liners.
2. Combine the coconut flour, baking soda, sea salt, almond flour and ground nuts; stir well.
3. Add the eggs and stir well.
4. Add stevia sweetener, coconut milk, almond milk and cacao chips; stir until all ingredients combine well.
5. Pour the coconut oil into muffin tins, three-fourths of each tin.
6. Pour the water into your Instant Pot and place a trivet.
7. Place muffin tin on a trivet and lock lid into place.
8. Set in the MANUAL setting for 5 minutes.
9. Serve hot.

Servings: 4

Cooking Times

Total Time: 10 minutes

Nutrition Facts

Serving size: 1/4 of a recipe (5 ounces)

Percent daily values based on the Reference Daily Intake (RDI) for a 2000 calorie diet.

Nutrition information calculated from recipe ingredients.

Amount Per Serving

Calories 124,97

Calories From Fat (56%) 70,12

% Daily Value

Total Fat 7,79g 12%

Saturated Fat 2,49g 12%

Cholesterol 279,82mg 93%

Sodium 281.67mg

Mini Greens Frittata

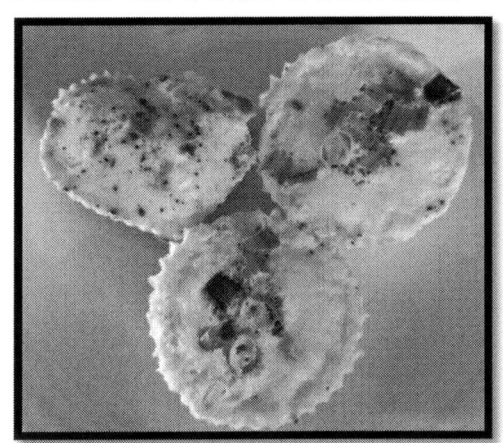

Ingredients

6 eggs

Splash of almond milk

1 green onion, finely chopped

Salt and pepper

1 cup water for Instant Pot

Instructions

1. Whisk eggs, milk, salt and pepper, and green onion in a bowl.
2. Pour mixture into individual silicone molds.
3. Place molds on a trivet in Instant Pot with 1 cup of water.
4. Lock lid into place and set on

the MANUAL setting for 5 minutes.

5. When the timer beeps, press "Cancel" and carefully flip the Quick Release valve to let the pressure out.

6. Serve hot.

Servings: 6

Cooking Times

Total Time: 10 minutes

Nutrition Facts

Serving size: 1/6 of a recipe (3.5 ounces)

Percent daily values based on the Reference Daily Intake (RDI) for a 2000 calorie diet.

Nutrition information calculated from recipe ingredients.

Amount Per Serving

Calories 104,39

Calories From Fat (55%) 57,04

% Daily Value

Total Fat 6,39g 10%

Saturated Fat 2,26g 11%

Cholesterol 187,18mg 62%

Mini Mushrooms Muffins

Ingredients

6 eggs

2 Tbsp almond milk

1 cup mushrooms, finely chopped

1/2 tsp garlic powder

Salt and pepper

1 cup water for Instant Pot

Instructions

1. Whisk eggs, milk, mushrooms, garlic powder, and salt and pepper in a bowl.
2. Pour the mixture into individual baking molds.
3. Pour water into your Instant Pot and place the trivet.
4. Place the baking molds on the trivet in your Instant Pot.
5. Lock lid into place and set on

the MANUAL setting for 15 minutes.
6. Release naturally pressure for 5 minutes and quick release remaining pressure.
7. Serve hot or cold.

Oysters and Mushrooms Frittata (Instant Pot)

Instructions

1 Tbsp lard

2 cups mushrooms, sliced

1/2 cup green onion, sliced

10 oysters, well drained

6 eggs

1 cup almond milk

1/4 tsp sweet paprika

1/4 tsp salt and ground pepper to taste

Instructions

1. Press SAUTÉ button on your Instant Pot and melt the lard.

Sauté mushrooms and onion for 3 minutes. Add oysters to mushroom mixture, and sauté for 1 - 2 minutes.

2. Whisk the eggs, milk, paprika, salt and pepper in a bowl. Pour the egg mixture over oyster mixture

3. Lock lid into place and set on the MANUAL setting for 5 minutes.

4. Use Natural Release.

5. Let sit for 5 minutes, cut into wedges and serve.

Power Almond Porridge (Instant Pot)

Ingredients

2 1/2 cups ground almonds soaked

1-quart water

3 cups almond milk (unsweetened)

10 whole almonds for decoration

1/2 cup Stevia sweetener or to taste

Instructions

1. Pour all ingredients from the list in your Instant Pot: stir well.
2. Lock lid into place and set on the PORRIDGE mode and adjust the time to 5 minutes.
3. When the timer beeps, press

"Cancel" and carefully flip the Quick Release valve to let the pressure out.

4. Serve with almonds and stevia sweetener to taste.

Servings: 10

Cooking Times

Total Time: 40 minutes

Nutrition Facts

Serving size: 1/10 of a recipe (2.5 ounces)

Percent daily values based on the Reference Daily Intake (RDI) for a 2000 calorie diet.

Nutrition information calculated from recipe ingredients.

Amount Per Serving

Calories 213,14

Calories From Fat (76%) 162,12

% Daily Value

Total Fat 18,75g 29%

Saturated Fat 3,78g 19%

Cholesterol 116,47mg 39%

Soft Almond Bread (Instant Pot)

Ingredients

6 large eggs (beaten)

1 tsp fresh lemon juice

1/4 cup lard

1 1/2 cup almond flour or ground almonds

3 tsp baking powder (gluten-free)

Pinch Sea salt to taste

2 cups water for Instant Pot

Instructions

1. Separate the egg whites from the yolks.
2. Add freshly squeezed lemon

juice to the whites and beat until soft peaks are achieved.

3. Combine the egg yolks, lard, almond flour, baking powder and salt in your food processor. Mix until combined well.
4. Add 1/3 of the egg whites to the almond flour mixture and process until mixed.
5. Add the remaining 2/3 of the egg whites and process until fully incorporated.
6. Pour mixture into a greased loaf pan.
7. Pour the water into your Instant Pot and place a trivet.
8. Place the loaf pan on a trivet and close the lid.
9. Lock lid into place and set on the MANUAL setting for 30 minutes.
10. Use Natural Release - it takes 10 - 25 minutes to depressurize naturally.
11. When ready, let cool, slice and serve.

Servings: 2

Cooking Times

Total Time: 10 minutes

Nutrition Facts

Serving size: 1/2 of a recipe (9.5 ounces)

Percent daily values based on the Reference Daily Intake (RDI) for a 2000 calorie diet.

Nutrition information calculated from recipe ingredients.

Amount Per Serving

Calories 125,48

Calories From Fat (71%) 89,54

% Daily Value

Total Fat 10,04g 15%

Saturated Fat 2,18g 11%

Cholesterol 186mg 62%

Steamed Eggs with Avocado Oil (instant Pot)

Ingredients

2 large eggs

2/3 cup cold water

1 Tbsp avocado oil

2 scallions, chopped

1/2 tsp garlic powder

Salt and ground pepper to taste

1 cup water for Instant Pot

Instructions

1. Whisk the eggs, avocado oil and water in a bowl.
2. Strain the egg mixture over a fine mesh strainer into 2 heat-

proof bowls.

3. Add finely chopped scallion, garlic powder and salt and pepper to taste; stir well.
4. Add 1 Cup of water to the inner pot of Instant Pot.
5. Place the trivet or steamer basket in the pot.
6. Place the bowl with the egg mixture on the trivet.
7. Lock lid into place and set on the MANUAL setting for 5 minutes.
8. Use Natural Release
9. Serve immediately.

Tomato-Poached Eggs (instant Pot)

Ingredients

1 Tbsp lard

1 large onion, finely diced

2 cloves garlic

3 tomatoes, peeled and grated

a few sprigs cilantro

1 tsp fresh parsley, finely chopped

1 tsp salt and ground black pepper to taste

4 eggs

Instructions

1. Press SAUTÉ button on your Instant Pot and heat the lard.

2. Add the onion and garlic with a pinch of salt and sauté for 3 minutes.
3. Add grated tomatoes and sauté, stirring, for about 2 - 3 minutes.
4. Add seasonings and stir well.
5. Crack the eggs over vegetables.
6. Lock lid into place and set on the MANUAL setting for 5 minutes.
7. When the timer beeps, press "Cancel" and carefully flip the Quick Release valve to let the pressure out.
8. Serve hot.

Servings: 5

Cooking Times

Preparation Time:
25 minutes

Nutrition Facts

Serving size: 1/5 of
a recipe (11
ounces)

Percent daily
values based on
the Reference Daily
Intake (RDI) for a
2000 calorie diet.

Nutrition
information
calculated from
recipe ingredients.

Amount Per
Serving

Calories 304,36

Calories From Fat
(23%) 71,19

% Daily Value

Total Fat 8,07g
12%

Saturated Fat 3,15g
16%

Cholesterol
117,4mg 39%

L U N C H

Braised Chicken Breast with Pearl Onions (Instant Pot)

Ingredients

1 Tbsp duck fat

2 lbs chicken breasts

1/2 lb Pearl onions (fresh)

2 cups carrots, chopped (fresh)

4 cloves garlic

3/4 cup water

1 tsp

Herbes de Provence (spice blend)

Salt and pepper to taste

3 Tbsp coconut milk

Instructions

1. Add duck fat in the inner cooker of your Instant Pot.
2. Place the chicken breast into the bottom, and add all remaining ingredients.
3. Lock lid into place and set in the POULTRY setting for 20 minutes.
4. When the timer beeps, press "Cancel" and carefully flip the Quick Release valve to let the pressure out.
5. Pour coconut milk and toss to combine well (do not stir).
6. Serve hot.

Servings: 8

Cooking Times

Total Time: 45 minutes

Nutrition Facts

Serving size: 1/8 of a recipe (13 ounces)

Percent daily values based on the Reference Daily Intake (RDI) for a 2000 calorie diet.

Nutrition information calculated from recipe ingredients.

Amount Per Serving

Calories 376,43

Calories From Fat (21%) 78,44

% Daily Value

Total Fat 8,83g 14%

Saturated Fat 2,55g 13%

Cholesterol 164,87mg 55%

Braised Turkey Breast with Orange Juice (Instant Pot)

Ingredients

2 Tbsp duck fat

4 lbs turkey breast

3 cups orange juice, freshly squeezed

1 cup water

1/2 tsp fresh rosemary, finely chopped

1/2 tsp fresh sage, finely chopped

1 tsp salt and ground red pepper to taste

Instructions

1. Fully submerge the turkey breast in the salted water and place it in the fridge for at least 4 to 8 hours.
2. Press SAUTÉ button on your Instant Pot and add the duck fat.
3. Brown the turkey breast from all sides.
4. Pour the orange juice and water and stir for 2 minutes.
5. Sprinkle with herbs, and salt and pepper and stir again.
6. Lock lid into place and set on the MANUAL high-pressure setting for 28 - 30 minutes.
7. Use Natural Release - it takes 10 - 25 minutes to depressurize naturally.
8. Use a meat thermometer to ensure the thickest part of the turkey breast registers over 161°F.
9. Serve hot.

Creamy Coco - Carrot Soup (Instant Pot)

Ingredients

1/4 cup Extra-virgin olive oil

1 cup scallion finely chopped

1 1/2 lb carrot, sliced 1/4 inch thick

4 cups water

1 Tbsp fresh dill, chopped

1 Tbsp fresh sage, chopped

Salt and pepper to taste

3/4 cup coconut milk (canned)

Instructions

1. Press SAUTÉ button on your Instant Pot and heat olive oil.

2. Sauté the scallions and carrots with a little salt.
3. Pour the water and add all remaining ingredients (except coconut milk); simmer for 2-3 minutes and stir.
4. Lock lid into place and set on the MANUAL setting for 10 minutes.
5. When the timer beeps, use Quick Release - turn the valve from sealing to venting to release the pressure.
6. Transfer your soup to a blender, add coconut milk and blend until creamy and soft.
7. Taste and adjust seasonings.
8. Serve immediately.

Creamy Cauliflower and Celery Soup (Instant Pot)

Ingredients

2 Tbsp lard

2 spring onions finely chopped

3 cups cauliflower, cut into bite-size pieces

4 stalks of celery, diced

2 Tbsp ground almonds, raw, without salt, added

1 ½ quart of water

Salt and freshly ground pepper

1 cup coconut milk (canned)

Instructions

1. Press the SAUTÉ button on

your Instant Pot and melt the lard. Sauté green onions for about 3 minutes.
2. Add all remaining ingredients and stir well.
3. Lock lid into place and set on the MANUAL setting for 10 minutes. Release pressure natural for 5 minutes and quick release remaining pressure.
4. Transfer soup in a blender, add coconut milk and pulse until soft and creamy.
5. Taste and adjust salt and pepper; stir. Serve hot.

Nutrition Facts

Serving size: 1/6 of a recipe (11.5 ounces)

Percent daily values based on the Reference Daily Intake (RDI) for a 2000 calorie diet.

Nutrition information calculated from recipe ingredients.

Amount Per Serving

Calories 379,3

Calories From Fat (27%) 103,08

% Daily Value

Total Fat 11,49g 18%

Saturated Fat 2,93g 15%

Cholesterol 197,09mg 66%

Easy Shredded Chicken (Instant Pot)

Ingredients

1/4 cup duck fat

4 lbs chicken breast

1 cup water

Sea salt and freshly ground white pepper

Instructions

1. Press SAUTÉ button on your Instant Pot and heat the duck fat.
2. Brown chicken from all sides.
3. Season the chicken with salt and pepper and pour the water.
4. Lock lid into place and set on

the "POULTRY" button, and add 15 minutes.

5. When the timer beeps, press "Cancel" and carefully flip the Quick Release valve to let the pressure out.

6. Transfer the chicken to a cutting board and use two forks to shred.

7. Serve hot or cold with your favorite seasonings.

Nutrition Facts

Serving size: 1/6 of a recipe (12 ounces)

Percent daily values based on the Reference Daily Intake (RDI) for a 2000 calorie diet.

Nutrition information calculated from recipe ingredients.

Amount Per Serving

Calories 315,37

Calories From Fat (77%) 242,15

% Daily Value

Total Fat 27,41g 42%

Saturated Fat 3,81g 19%

Cholesterol 0mg 0%

Greek Okra with Grated Tomatoes (Instant Pot)

Ingredients

3/4 cup Extra-virgin olive oil

1 onion, finely diced

2 cloves garlic, minced

2 carrots sliced

2 lbs okra

4 ripe tomatoes grated

Salt and ground black pepper

1 cup water

1 Tbsp fresh parsley, finely chopped

Instructions

1. Press SAUTÉ button on your Instant Pot and heat the oil.
2. Sauté the onion and garlic for about 3 minutes or until soft.
3. Add the carrot and okra and stir for 2 minutes.
4. Add grated tomatoes, salt, and pepper and cook for 2 minutes; stir.
5. Pour water, stir well and lock lid into place.
6. Use Natural Release for 5 minutes and quick release remaining pressure.
7. Taste and adjust salt and pepper.
8. Sprinkle with chopped parsley and serve immediately.

Green Beans Soup with Herbs (Instant Pot)

Ingredients

1 Tbsp lard

1 large onion, chopped

1 1/2 lbs. green beans, frozen

1 can (15 oz) diced tomatoes

2 cups water

1 cup fresh parsley, finely chopped

1 tsp dried oregano and thyme, crumbled

Salt and ground pepper to taste

Instructions

1. Press SAUTÉ button on your Instant Pot and add the lard and chopped onion in your

Instant Pot.

2. Sauté the onion stirring occasionally, until softened, for about 2-3 minutes.
3. Add all remaining ingredients and stir well.
4. Lock lid into place and set on the MANUAL setting for 4-5 minutes.
5. When the timer beeps, naturally release pressure for 5 minutes and quick release remaining pressure.
6. Adjust seasonings and serve hot.

Servings: 6

Cooking Times

Total Time: 25 minutes

Nutrition Facts

Serving size: 1/6 of a recipe (12 ounces)

Percent daily values based on the Reference Daily Intake (RDI) for a 2000 calorie diet.

Nutrition information calculated from recipe ingredients.

Amount Per Serving

Calories 281,71

Calories From Fat (66%) 186,9

% Daily Value

Total Fat 20,43g 31%

Saturated Fat 6,96g 35%

Cholesterol 56,7mg 19%

Ground Beef and Cabbage Soup

Ingredients

2 Tbsp Extra-virgin olive oil

1/2 cup chopped onion

1 tsp garlic, minced

1 cup chopped carrots

1 lb ground beef

1 can (15 oz) diced tomatoes

3 cups cabbage, coarsely chopped

1 cup chopped celery

2 cups water

1 Tbsp white vinegar

1 tsp chili powder

Kosher salt and ground black pepper

Instructions

1. Press SAUTÉ button on your Instant Pot and heat the oil.
2. Sauté the onion and garlic for 2 - 3 minutes or until soft
3. Add carrots and sauté for about 2 minutes; stir.
4. Add ground beef and diced tomatoes; stir for 2 minutes.
5. Add all remaining ingredients, give a good stir and close the lid.
6. Lock lid into place and set on the MANUAL setting for 8 minutes.
7. Use Natural Release - it takes 10 - 25 minutes to depressurize naturally.
8. Taste and adjust seasonings.
9. Serve.

Servings: 4

Cooking Times

Total Time: 30 minutes

Nutrition Facts

Serving size: 1/4 of a recipe (7.5 ounces)

Percent daily values based on the Reference Daily Intake (RDI) for a 2000 calorie diet.

Nutrition information calculated from recipe ingredients.

Amount Per Serving

Calories 109,86

Calories From Fat (57%) 62,29

% Daily Value

Total Fat 7,06g 11%

Saturated Fat 0,96g 5%

Cholesterol 0mg 0%

Hot Radish Greens Salad (Instant Pot)

Ingredients

2 Tbsp Extra-virgin olive oil

1 onion, finely sliced

3 cloves garlic (finely minced)

1 lb fresh radish greens, chopped

1/2 cup water

2 Tbsp tomato puree

3 tsp lemon juice freshly squeezed

1/2 tsp salt and ground black pepper to taste

Instructions

1. Wash and clean radish greens.
2. Remove the thickest parts of

the stems at the base of greens. Chop the stems into small pieces.

3. Press SAUTÉ button on your Instant Pot and heat the oil.
4. Sauté the green onions and garlic with a pinch of salt for 2 - 3 minutes.
5. Add the radish greens and sauté, stirring occasionally, for 2 minutes.
6. Add all remaining ingredients, season salt, and pepper.
7. Lock lid into place and set on the MANUAL setting for 11 - 12 minutes.
8. When the timer beeps, press "Cancel" and carefully flip the Quick Release valve to let the pressure out.
9. Taste and adjust seasonings to taste.
10. Serve with extra lemon juice.

Cooking Times

Total Time: 25 minutes

Nutrition Facts

Serving size: 1/4 of a recipe (12 ounces)

Percent daily values based on the Reference Daily Intake (RDI) for a 2000 calorie diet.

Nutrition information calculated from recipe ingredients.

Amount Per Serving

Calories 212,07

Calories From Fat (45%) 95,4

% Daily Value

Total Fat 10,83g 17%

Saturated Fat 1,57g 8%

Cholesterol 0mg

Mango Cabbage Slaw (Instant Pot)

Ingredients

3 Tbsp olive oil

2 onions, finely sliced

4 cups pickled cabbage shredded

1 carrot, grated

2 mangos chopped

1 Tbsp lemon juice, or to taste

Salt and pepper to taste

Instructions

1. Press SAUTÉ button on your Instant Pot and heat the oil.
2. Sauté the onions with a pinch of salt for 2 - 3 minutes.
3. Add the cabbage and sauté,

stirring often, for 3 - 4 minutes.

4. Add all remaining ingredients and stir well.
5. Lock lid into place and set on the MANUAL setting for 12 minutes.
6. When the timer beeps, press "Cancel" and carefully flip the Quick Release valve to let the pressure out.
7. Taste and adjust salt and pepper to taste.
8. Pour some lemon juice (if used) and serve immediately.

Mottled Vegetable Soup (Instant Pot)

Ingredients

2 Tbsp olive oil

2 onions, chopped

3 cloves garlic

2 carrots, peeled and cut into chunks

1 red bell pepper cut into chunks

1/2 head of cabbage, chopped

3 zucchini cut into chunks

4 cups water

Salt and black ground pepper to taste

1 Tbsp fresh basil and rosemary, finely chopped

1 tsp cayenne pepper

1 tsp fresh thyme and oregano finely chopped

Instructions

1. Wash and chop your vegetables.
2. Press SAUTÉ button on your Instant Pot and heat the oil.
3. Add the onion and garlic and sauté for 2 minutes.
4. Add carrots and pepper and sauté for 2 minutes; stir well.
5. Place all remaining ingredients, stir well; close lid and the release valve.
6. Set in the MANUAL setting for 5 minutes.
7. When done, use Quick Release - turn the valve from sealing to venting to release the pressure.
8. Taste and adjust seasonings
9. Serve hot in soup bowls.

Servings: 4

Cooking Times

Total Time: 50 minutes

Nutrition Facts

Serving size: 1/4 of a recipe (10 ounces)

Percent daily values based on the Reference Daily Intake (RDI) for a 2000 calorie diet.

Nutrition information calculated from recipe ingredients.

Amount Per Serving

Calories 260,78

Calories From Fat (33%) 86,01

% Daily Value

Total Fat 9,68g 15%

Saturated Fat 1,46g 7%

Cholesterol 97,5mg 33%

Perch Fillets with Garlic (Instant Pot)

Ingredients

1 1/2 lb perch fillets

2 Tbsp Extra-virgin olive oil

1 onion, finely diced

4 cloves garlic, minced

3/4 cup dry white wine

Instructions

1. Season perch fillets with salt and rub with minced garlic. Set aside.
2. Press SAUTÉ button on your Instant Pot and heat the oil.
3. Sauté the onion for two minutes until soft.
4. Add garlic and sauté for one

minute more.
5. Season with the salt and pepper.
6. Add the perch fillets and lock lid into place; set on the MANUAL setting for 6 minutes.
7. When the timer beeps, press "Cancel" and carefully flip the Quick Release valve to let the pressure out.
8. Serve hot.

Servings: 6

Cooking Times

Total Time: 25 minutes

Nutrition Facts

Serving size: 1/6 of a recipe (12 ounces)

Percent daily values based on the Reference Daily Intake (RDI) for a 2000 calorie diet.

Nutrition information calculated from recipe ingredients.

Amount Per Serving

Calories 77,77

Calories From Fat (8%) 5,98

% Daily Value

Total Fat 0,72g 1%

Saturated Fat 0,13g <1%

Cholesterol 0mg 0%

Pumpkin Soup with Curry and Apple (Instant Pot)

Ingredients

2 Tbsp of Extra-virgin olive oil

1 onion, finely chopped

1 carrot, finely chopped

1 1/2 lbs pumpkin, cut into cubes

1 large sweet potato, cut into cubes

2 apples, cut into cubes

4 cups water

1 - 2 Tbsp fresh lemon juice

1 Tbsp curry

1 Tbsp cumin

1 tsp coriander

1 tsp dill

1/2 tsp coriander

Salt and ground pepper to taste

Instructions

1. Press SAUTÉ button on your Instant Pot and heat the oil.
2. Add the onion and carrot and sauté for 2 - 3 minutes.
3. Add sweet potato and apples and stir for one minute.
4. Add the pumpkin cubes and give a good stir.
5. Pour water and close the lid.
6. Lock lid into place and set on the MANUAL setting for 12 minutes.
7. When the timer beeps, press Natural Release.
8. Pour the pumpkin mixtures in batches in your food processor or fast-speed blender.
9. Pour the lemon juice, curry, cumin, coriander, dill and salt and ground pepper to taste.
10. Blend until completely smooth.
11. Serve immediately.

Nutrition Facts

Serving size: 1/6 of a recipe (10 ounces)

Percent daily values based on the Reference Daily Intake (RDI) for a 2000 calorie diet.

Nutrition information calculated from recipe ingredients.

Amount Per Serving

Calories 126,59

Calories From Fat (33%) 42,22

% Daily Value

Total Fat 4,75g 7%

Saturated Fat 0,91g 5%

Cholesterol 32.27mg 11%

Silky Seafood Soup with Dill (Instant Pot)

Ingredients

1 Tbsp Extra-virgin olive oil

1 Tbsp onion finely chopped

2 bay leaves

4 1/2 cups of water

1 carrot cut into cubes

2 stalk of celery, cleaned, cut into cubes

2 Tbsp yellow mustard

1 tsp fresh thyme, finely chopped

1 tsp lemon peel

1 tsp cumin

2 raw shrimp without shell

5 oz fish fillet cut into pieces

Salt and ground pepper to taste

Fresh dill, finely chopped, for serving

Instructions

1. Pour oil into your Instant Pot and add all remaining ingredients. Stir to combine well.
2. Lock lid into place and set on the MANUAL setting for 8 minutes.
3. Use Natural Release - it takes 10 - 25 minutes to depressurize naturally.
4. Remove bay leaves and transfer the soup to your blender. Beat until smooth.
5. Taste and adjust seasonings.
6. Warm again and serve with chopped dill.

Steamed Carrot and Broccoli (Instant Pot)

Ingredients

2 Tbsp Extra-virgin olive oil

2 cups carrots, sliced

1 head broccoli, cut into florets

2 leeks, chopped

3 cups water

Salt and white pepper to taste

Instructions

1. Pour the oil into your Instant Pot.
2. Add all remaining ingredients.
3. Lock lid into place and set on the MANUAL setting for 5 minutes.
4. Open the lid and transfer vegetables on serving plate.
5. Serve hot

DINNER

"Roasted" Brussels sprouts with Bacon (Instant Pot)

Ingredients

2 lbs of Brussels sprouts

1/4 cup olive oil

Salt and pepper to taste

6 slices bacon, cut into pieces

1 cup water

Instructions

1. Rinse the Brussels sprouts in cold water to remove any dust or dirt.

64

2. Using a sharp knife, take off the tip of the stem and discard it.
3. Place the sprouts in your Instant Pot and pour evenly with olive oil.
4. Season with the salt and pepper.
5. Add the chopped bacon evenly over the Brussels sprouts.
6. Lock lid into place and set on the MANUAL setting for 3 minutes.
7. When the timer beeps, press "Cancel" and carefully flip the Quick Release valve to let the pressure out.
8. Serve immediately.

Servings: 4

Cooking Times

Total Time: 15 minutes

Nutrition Facts

Serving size: 1/4 of a recipe (13 ounces)

Percent daily values based on the Reference Daily Intake (RDI) for a 2000 calorie diet.

Nutrition information calculated from recipe ingredients.

Amount Per Serving

Calories 242,15

Calories From Fat (39%) 93,35

% Daily Value

Total Fat 10,52g 16%

Saturated Fat 2,27g 11%

Cholesterol 62,37mg 21%

Beef, Zucchini and Pepper Stew (Instant Pot)

Ingredients

2 Tbsp olive oil

1 lb ground beef

3 zucchini, diced

2 mild chili peppers, diced

2 small tomatoes, peeled and chopped

2 cups water

1 cup mashed sweet potato

2 tsp dried oregano

2 tsp garlic powder

Salt and fresh-ground black pepper to taste

Instructions

1. Pour the olive oil into your Instant Pot.
2. Place all ingredients in your Instant Pot and toss to combine well.
3. Lock lid into place and set on the MANUAL setting for 6 minutes.
4. Release pressure natural for 5 minutes and quick release remaining pressure.
5. Carefully open the lid.
6. Taste and adjust seasonings; stir.
7. Serve hot.

Servings: 5

Cooking Times

Total Time: 15 minutes

Nutrition Facts

Serving size: 1/5 of a recipe (12, ounces)

Percent daily values based on the Reference Daily Intake (RDI) for a 2000 calorie diet.

Nutrition information calculated from recipe ingredients.

Amount Per Serving

Calories 191,36

Calories From Fat (52%) 100,25

% Daily Value

Total Fat 11,37g 17%

Saturated Fat 1,63g 8%

Cholesterol 0mg 0%

Cabbage and Carrots in Tomato Sauce (Instant Pot)

Ingredients

1/4 cup olive oil

1 large onion, chopped

4 cloves garlic, minced

1 head cabbage, chopped

3 carrots, sliced

3 tomatoes, peeled

2 tsp all-spice

1/2 tsp cinnamon

Salt and ground pepper to taste

Instructions

1. Rinse and wash the cabbage.
2. With the knife, cut the cabbage head in half and then into wedges.
3. Pour the oil into your Instant Pot and Select SAUTÉ setting; sauté the onion, garlic, and carrot until soft.
4. Season salt and pepper and stir well.
5. Place cabbage wedges in your Instant Pot (3/4 of the pot).
6. Pour diced tomatoes and stir to combine. Sprinkle all-spices and cinnamon and stir well.
7. Press CANCEL and lock lid into place; set on the MANUAL setting for 5 minutes.
8. Release pressure natural for 15 minutes and quick release remaining pressure.
9. Serve hot.

Chinese Ginger-Turmeric Tilapia (Instant Pot)

Ingredients

2 cups of water for Instant Pot

1 1/2 tsp fresh ginger, grated

1/2 tsp turmeric ground

2 lb Tilapia fish

Sea salt and black ground pepper to taste

3 Tbsp Garlic-infused Olive oil

1 lemon

Instructions

1. In the inner liner of your Instant Pot, place 2 cups of water and a steaming basket fitted for the pressure cooker. Pour grated ginger and

turmeric in water.

2. Season Tilapia fish with salt and pepper, and garlic-infused Olive oil. Place the fish in a steaming basket.
3. Lock lid into place and set on the MANUAL setting for 4 minutes.
4. Use Quick Release. Serve hot with lemon slices.

Servings: 6

Cooking Times

Total Time: 20
minutes

Nutrition Facts

Serving size: 1/6 of a
recipe (11 ounces)

Percent daily values
based on the
Reference Daily
Intake (RDI) for a
2000 calorie diet.

Nutrition information
calculated from
recipe ingredients.

Amount Per Serving

Calories 148,41

Calories From Fat
(58%) 85,52

% Daily Value

Total Fat 9,7g 15%

Saturated Fat 1,38g
7%

Cholesterol 0mg 0%

Sodium 43,6mg 2%

Potassium 705,14mg
20%

Total Carbohydrates

Classic Ratatouille (Instant Pot)

Ingredients

1/4 cup olive oil

1 onion, chopped

2 tsp minced garlic

4 tomatoes, peeled and chopped

1 red bell peppers, chopped

1 green bell peppers, chopped

2 zucchini, chopped

1 eggplant, cubed

2 Tbsp fresh basil, chopped

2 Tbsp fresh parsley, finely chopped

Sea salt to taste

Instructions

1. Wash and chop all vegetables.
2. Press SAUTÉ button on your Instant Pot and heat the oil.
3. Sauté the onion and garlic until soft.
4. Add all other ingredients and press "Keep Warm/Cancel".
5. Lock lid into place and set on the MANUAL setting for 6 minutes.
6. Release pressure natural for 5 minutes and quick release remaining pressure.
7. Taste and adjust seasonings.
8. Serve immediately.

Nutrition Facts

Serving size: 1/6 of a recipe (12 ounces)

Percent daily values based on the Reference Daily Intake (RDI) for a 2000 calorie diet.

Nutrition information calculated from recipe ingredients.

Amount Per Serving

Calories 124,82

Calories From Fat (7%) 8,92

% Daily Value

Total Fat 1,01g 2%

Saturated Fat 0,2g 1%

Cholesterol 48.76mg 16%

Codfish and Cauliflower Stew (Instant Pot)

Ingredients

3 Tbsp olive oil

1 onion, chopped

2 cloves garlic, chopped

1 carrot, chopped

2 fresh tomatoes, piled and diced

3 tsp fresh parsley, chopped

1/2 tsp sweet paprika

3 1/2 cup water

1 1/2 lb cod fish, boneless

2 cups cauliflower florets, diced

Salt and freshly ground pepper to taste

Instructions

1. Cut the fish it into small chunks.
2. Heat the olive oil in a frying pan, and sauté the onion and garlic until soft.
3. Add the carrots and parsley and sauté for 2 minutes; stir.
4. Add in chopped tomatoes and cook for only one minute; stir well.
5. Transfer mixture in your Instant Pot.
6. Add the fish and cauliflower.
7. Season with the paprika, salt, and pepper to taste and pour the water.
8. Lock lid into place and set on the MANUAL setting for 5 minutes.
9. When the timer beeps, press "Cancel" and carefully flip the Quick Release valve to let the pressure out.
10. Taste and adjust salt and black pepper. Serve hot.

Servings: 4

Cooking Times

Total Time: 20 minutes

Nutrition Facts

Serving size: 1/4 of a recipe (13 ounces)

Percent daily values based on the Reference Daily Intake (RDI) for a 2000 calorie diet.

Nutrition information calculated from recipe ingredients.

Amount Per Serving

Calories 496,1

Calories From Fat (70%) 349,45

% Daily Value

Total Fat 38,72g 60%

Saturated Fat 15,02g 75%

Cholesterol 85,05mg 28%

Ground Beef and Eggplant with Basil (Instant Pot)

Ingredients

3 Tbsp extra-virgin olive oil

2 green onions, diced

2 cloves garlic, chopped

1 lb ground beef

1 large eggplant, cut into thin cubes

1 cup tomatoes, peeled and finely chopped

½ cup fresh basil, diced

Salt and ground pepper to taste

3 cup coconut milk, canned

Instructions

1. Heat olive oil in a large pan over medium-high heat.
2. Add the green onions and garlic. Sauté for 3 - 4 minutes, until soft.
3. Add the ground beef and cook until brown.
4. Place ground beef mixture in your greased Instant Pot.
5. Add all remaining ingredients, and season with the salt and a pepper.
6. Lock lid into place and set on the MANUAL setting for 6 minutes.
7. Use Natural Release for 5 minutes and quick release remaining pressure.
8. Taste and adjust salt and pepper.
9. Serve immediately and garnish with fresh basil.
10. Discard liquid (and fat that drained off beef) from your Instant Pot Base.

Jumbo Shrimp Soup (Instant Pot)

Ingredients

2 Tbsp olive oil

2 scallions finely chopped

1 piece fresh ginger, grated

Kosher salt and freshly ground white pepper

1 tsp fresh parsley finely chopped

1/2 tsp ground sweet paprika

1/2 tsp dill chopped

15 oz jumbo shrimp, unpeeled

6 cups water

Instructions

1. Press SAUTÉ button on your Instant Pot and heat the oil.
2. Cook scallions for 3 - 4 minutes or until soft.
3. Add all remaining ingredients and stir well.
4. Lock lid into place and set on the MANUAL setting for 2 - 3 minutes.
5. When the timer beeps, press "Cancel" and carefully flip the Quick Release valve to let the pressure out.
6. Taste and adjust seasonings.
7. Sprinkle with chopped parsley and serve hot.

Servings: 4

Octopus with Peppers and Mustard (Instant Pot)

Ingredients

1 medium octopus (about 1 lb)

1 cup water

2 bay leaves

1/2 tsp sweet paprika powder

1 tsp red hot paprika

Salt and ground pepper

1/4 cup garlic-infused olive oil

1 onion, finely chopped

1 red sweet pepper cut into strips

1 orange sweet pepper cut into strips

1 cup yellow mustard (without alcohol)

Instructions

1. Place the octopus, bay leaves, sweet paprika powder, red-hot paprika, and salt and pepper and in your Instant Pot.
2. Lock lid into place and set on the MANUAL setting for 10 minutes.
3. Use Natural Release for 5 minutes and quick release remaining pressure.
4. Remove the octopus from the pot, and cut into cubes.
5. Heat the olive oil in a large frying skillet over medium-high heat.
6. Sauté the onion with peppers with a pinch of salt until soft.
7. Add the octopus cubes and mustard. Simmer until all liquids evaporate.
8. Taste and adjust seasonings.
9. Serve hot.

Servings: 6

Cooking Times

Total Time: 40 minutes

Nutrition Facts

Serving size: 1/6 of a recipe (10 ounces)

Percent daily values based on the Reference Daily Intake (RDI) for a 2000 calorie diet.

Nutrition information calculated from recipe ingredients.

Amount Per Serving

Calories 296,38

Calories From Fat (71%) 211,48

% Daily Value

Total Fat 23,62g 36%

Saturated Fat 6,47g 32%

Cholesterol 24,74mg 8%

Pork with Eggplants and Peppers (Instant Pot)

Ingredients

3 Tbsp Olive oil

2 spring onions finely chopped

2 cloves garlic

2 red sweet bell peppers

2 lbs eggplants cut into slices

1 tomato, peeled, seeded, and chopped

1/2 lb pork cut into cubes

1/2 tsp sea salt and ground pepper to taste

1 tsp red crushed pepper

1/2 tsp thyme leaves finely chopped

1/2 cup water

Instructions

1. Clean and cut eggplants into large slices. Rub the eggplant slices with sea salt and place in a colander to drain.
2. Place the colander over a large bowl or in a sink.
3. Carefully rinse each piece of eggplant under cold water, making sure you remove all the salt. Set aside.
4. Press SAUTÉ button on your Instant Pot and pour the oil.
5. Cook the onion, garlic, peppers, eggplant and tomato for 3 - 4 minutes or until soft.
6. Add the pork cubes and cook for about 2 - 3 minutes; stir.
7. Season the salt and pepper, thyme leaves finely and red crushed pepper; stir well.
8. Lock lid into place and set on the MANUAL setting for 20 minutes.
9. Use Natural Release for 5 minutes and quick release remaining pressure.
10. Taste and adjust salt and pepper to taste.
11. Serve hot.

Servings: 4

Cooking Times

Inactive Time: 30 minutes

Cooking Time: 10 minutes

Nutrition Facts

Serving size: 1/4 of a recipe (9 ounces)

Percent daily values based on the Reference Daily Intake (RDI) for a 2000 calorie diet.

Nutrition information calculated from recipe ingredients.

Amount Per Serving

Calories 192,33

Calories From Fat (7%) 14,34

% Daily Value

Total Fat 1,59g 2%

Saturated Fat 0,33g 2%

Cholesterol 99.33mg 33%

Saffron-marinated Cod Fillets (Instant Pot)

Ingredients

4 Cod fillets without skin

1/4 cup virgin olive oil

Pinch of saffron threads

2 splash of apple vinegar

Fresh basil, finely chopped, for garnish

1/2 tsp sea salt and black pepper or to taste

1 cup water

Instructions

1. Combine the olive oil, saffron threads, salt, pepper and vinegar in a shallow dish.

2. Add the fish fillets and toss well to coat.
3. Grind over some extra pepper, cover and leave to marinate in the fridge for 30 minutes.
4. Pour water into your Instant Pot and place the steaming basket.
5. Place fish on the steaming basket.
6. Lock lid into place and set on the MANUAL setting for 5 minutes.
7. Use Quick Release - turn the valve from sealing to venting to release the pressure.
8. Serve hot garnished with chopped basil.

Servings: 8

Cooking Times

Total Time: 1 hour
and 5 minutes

Nutrition Facts

Serving size: 1/8 of a
recipe (11.5 ounces)

Percent daily values
based on the
Reference Daily
Intake (RDI) for a
2000 calorie diet.

Nutrition information
calculated from
recipe ingredients.

Amount Per Serving

Calories 518,22

Calories From Fat
(58%) 299,63

% Daily Value

Total Fat 32,62g 50%

Saturated Fat 12,33g
62%

Cholesterol
115,67mg 39%

Sodium 127,9mg 5%

Potassium
1037,36mg 30%

Total Carbohydrates

Seasoned Beef with Potatoes (Instant Pot)

Ingredients

2 Tbsp olive oil

3 lbs beef chuck roast, boneless

1 large onion, cut into wedges

4 potatoes, sliced

3 carrots, sliced

1 1/2 cups water

1/2 tsp marjoram

1/2 tsp nutmeg

1/2 tsp sage

1/2 tsp sea salt and ground black pepper to taste

Instructions

1. Season meat generously with the salt and pepper.
2. Pour the oil into your Instant Pot.
3. Place the meat and press SAUTÉ button setting; brown meat from all sides, for about two minutes.
4. Add the onion, sliced carrots, and potatoes.
5. Add marjoram, nutmeg, sage and salt and pepper.
6. Pour water and stir well.
7. Lock lid into place and set on the "MEAT/STEW" setting for 35 minutes.
8. When the timer beeps, use Natural Release.
9. Transfer the roast and vegetables to a serving dish. Serve hot.

Servings: 8

Cooking Times

Total Time: 45 minutes

Nutrition Facts

Serving size: 1/8 of a recipe (12 ounces)

Percent daily values based on the Reference Daily Intake (RDI) for a 2000 calorie diet.

Nutrition information calculated from recipe ingredients.

Amount Per Serving

Calories 302,79

Calories From Fat (5%) 15,25

% Daily Value

Total Fat 1,71g 3%

Saturated Fat 0,51g 3%

Cholesterol 140,62mg 47%

Sodium 113.22mg

Spicy Turkey Breast (Instant Pot)

Ingredients

4 lbs turkey breast

3 cups orange juice, freshly squeezed

1 Tbsp honey

1 cup water

1/2 tsp dried rosemary

1/4 tsp dried thyme

1/4 tsp garlic powder

1/4 tsp hot paprika

1 tsp salt and ground red pepper

Instructions

1. Season your turkey breasts with salt.
2. Press SAUTÉ button on your Instant Pot and brown the turkey breast from all sides.
3. Whisk together the orange juice, water, rosemary, thyme, garlic, hot paprika and salt and red ground pepper.
4. Pour the orange mixture over turkey breasts.
5. Lock lid into place and set on the MANUAL setting for 30 minutes or until turkey breasts are soft and fully cooked (internal temperature reaches 165°F).
6. After the cooking time is over, use naturally release for 5 minutes and quick release remaining pressure.
7. Serve hot.

Servings: 4

Cooking Times

Total Time: 10 minutes

Nutrition Facts

Serving size: 1/4 of a recipe (14 ounces)

Percent daily values based on the Reference Daily Intake (RDI) for a 2000 calorie diet.

Nutrition information calculated from recipe ingredients.

Amount Per Serving

Calories 467,76

Calories From Fat (13%) 60,51

% Daily Value

Total Fat 6,73g 10%

Saturated Fat 1,48g 7%

Cholesterol 245mg 82%

Steamed Flounder with Scallions and Cilantro (Instant Pot)

Ingredients

4 flounder filets

4 scallions

2 Tbsp fresh ginger, grated

2 bunch of cilantro

1 tsp garlic powder

1/2 tsp onion powder

Salt and ground black pepper to taste

Instructions

1. Wash, clean and julienne scallions, ginger, and cilantro.
2. Place your steaming basket

90

and 2 cups of water into your Instant Pot.

3. Place the flounder fish on a steaming basket in your Instant Pot.
4. Place scallions, ginger, and cilantro over the fish.
5. Sprinkle garlic and onion powder and salt and pepper.
6. Lock lid into place and set on the STEAM setting for 5 minutes.
7. When the timer beeps, press "Cancel" and carefully flip the Quick Release valve to let the pressure out.
8. Serve hot.

Steamed Tilapia Fillets with Garlic (Instant Pot)

Ingredients

2 Tbsp olive oil

2 1/2 lbs fresh tilapia fillets

Sea salt to taste

6 garlic cloves, finely sliced

1 - 2 lemons, for serving

2 cups water (for Instant Pot)

Fresh parsley (for garnish)

Instructions

1. Season the fish with the salt from all sides; grease the fish.
2. In the inner liner of your Instant Pot, place 2 cups of water and a steamer. Place the fish in a steamer basket. Sprinkle fish generously with

finely chopped garlic.

3. Lock lid into place and set on the MANUAL setting for 3 minutes.

4. Use Natural Release for 5 minutes and quick release remaining pressure.

5. Serve with freshly squeezed lemon juice and garnish with chopped parsley.

Servings: 4

Cooking Times

Total Time: 25 minutes

Nutrition Facts

Serving size: 1/4 of a recipe (11 ounces)

Percent daily values based on the Reference Daily Intake (RDI) for a 2000 calorie diet.

Nutrition information calculated from recipe ingredients.

Amount Per Serving

Calories 305,47

Calories From Fat (39%) 119,61

% Daily Value

Total Fat 13,72g 21%

Saturated Fat 1,72g 9%

Cholesterol 0mg 0%

SIDE DISH

"Roasted" Pesto Potatoes (Instant Pot)

Ingredients

3 Tbsp Extra-virgin olive oil

2 lbs medium potatoes

4 Tbsp fresh basil leaves, finely chopped

2 cloves garlic, melted

3 Tbsp ground almonds

Salt and ground black pepper to taste

1 cup water

Instructions

1. Clean, wash and slice potatoes.
2. Press SAUTÉ button on your Instant Pot.
3. When the word "HOT" appears on the display add the oil.
4. Sauté the potatoes with a pinch of salt, for about 5 - 6 minutes.
5. Stir with a wooden spoon all the time.
6. Add the basil, melted garlic, ground almonds and salt and pepper to taste.
7. Pour the water and stir well.
8. Lock lid into place and set on the MANUAL setting for 11 minutes.
9. Use Quick Release - turn the valve from sealing to venting to release the pressure.
10. Serve hot.

"Roasted" Red Potatoes with Garlic (Instant Pot)

Servings: 4

Cooking Times

Cooking Time: 1 hour

Total Time: 25 minutes

Nutrition Facts

Serving size: 1/4 of a recipe (10 ounces)

Percent daily values based on the Reference Daily Intake (RDI) for a 2000 calorie diet.

Nutrition information calculated from recipe ingredients.

Amount Per Serving

Calories 310,34

Calories From Fat (39%) 122,11

% Daily Value

Total Fat 13,82g 21%

Saturated Fat 1,93g 10%

Ingredients

1/4 cup extra virgin olive oil

8 cloves garlic, thinly sliced

2 lbs red potatoes, cut into chunks

2 tsp fresh rosemary, finely chopped

2 tsp fresh thyme, finely chopped

Kosher salt and ground black pepper to taste

1/4 cup water

Instructions

1. Press SAUTÉ button on your Instant Pot.
2. When the word "hot" appears on the display, add the oil and

sauté the garlic for about 4 - 5 minutes.

3. Add red potatoes and stir for 5 minutes. Add all remaining ingredients and stir well.
4. Lock lid into place and set on the MANUAL setting for 11 minutes.
5. Use Natural Release for 5 minutes and quick release remaining pressure. Serve hot.

Servings: 8

Cooking Times

Total Time: 20 minutes

Nutrition Facts

Serving size: 1/8 of a recipe (5 ounces)

Percent daily values based on the Reference Daily Intake (RDI) for a 2000 calorie diet.

Nutrition information calculated from recipe ingredients.

Amount Per Serving

Calories 41,14

Calories From Fat (6%) 2,63

% Daily Value

Total Fat 0,31g <1%

Saturated Fat 0,06g <1%

Cholesterol 0mg 0%

Sodium 465.11mg

Fresh Tomatoes Marinara Sauce (Instant Pot)

Ingredients

4 Tbsp Extra-virgin olive oil

1 onion, finely chopped

2 cloves garlic, minced

1 1/2 lb fresh tomatoes peeled and finely chopped (or grated)

1 can (6 oz) tomato paste

1 tsp dried oregano

4 Tbsp chopped fresh parsley

1 tsp salt and ground black pepper

1/2 cup water

Instructions

1. Press SAUTÉ button on your

Instant Pot and heat the oil.
2. Add the onion and garlic and sauté until soft.
3. Add all remaining ingredients in your Instant Pot; stir well.
4. Lock lid into place and set on the MANUAL setting for 10 minutes.
5. When the timer beeps, press "Cancel" and carefully flip the Quick Release valve to let the pressure out.
6. Transfer the mixture and puree in batches in a regular blender and return to the pot.
7. Press sauté function again and stir for 2 - 3 minutes.
8. Taste and adjust seasonings.
9. Serve or keep in a glass jar in refrigerator.

Green Garden Cream Dip (Instant Pot)

Ingredients

3 Tbsp olive oil

1 onion, finely chopped

2 cloves garlic, minced

1 lb broccoli

3 stalks celery, chopped

1 apple, cored and chopped

2 potatoes

2 cups water

1 Tbsp ginger grated

1 tsp curry powder

Salt and ground black pepper to taste

Instructions

1. Press SAUTÉ button on your Instant Pot.
2. When the word "HOT" appears on the display, add the oil and sauté the onions and garlic about 5 minutes.
3. Add all remaining ingredients and stir well.
4. Lock lid into place and set on the MANUAL setting for 10 minutes.
5. When the beep sounds, quick release the pressure by pressing Cancel, and twisting the steam handle to the Venting position.
6. Transfer soup to a blender and blend until smooth.
7. Taste and adjust seasonings.

Servings: 6

Cooking Times

Total Time: 15 minutes

Nutrition Facts

Serving size: 1/6 of a recipe (9 ounces)

Percent daily values based on the Reference Daily Intake (RDI) for a 2000 calorie diet.

Nutrition information calculated from recipe ingredients.

Amount Per Serving

Calories 137,96

Calories From Fat (59%) 80,94

% Daily Value

Total Fat 9,54g 15%

Saturated Fat 1,15g 6%

Cholesterol 0mg 0%

Sodium 724.02mg

Green Olives Cream with Almonds (Instant Pot)

Ingredients

2 cups green olives, pitted and chopped

1 lb zucchini, sliced

1 tomato, peeled and grated

3 cloves garlic, minced

2 tsp capers

1 Tbsp fresh basil, finely chopped

Salt and pepper, to taste

1/2 cup water

3 Tbsp almonds ground

Instructions

1. Prepare the olives and vegetables.

2. Place the olives, zucchini, grated tomato, garlic, capers, fresh basil, water and salt and pepper in your Instant Pot; stir well.
3. Lock lid into place and set on the MANUAL setting for 5 minutes.
4. Use Natural Release for 10 minutes and quick release remaining pressure.
5. Transfer olive mixture to your blender and add ground almonds. Blend until combine well.
6. Serve immediately or keep refrigerated.

Total Time: 20 minutes

Nutrition Facts

Serving size: 1/4 of a recipe (9 ounces)

Percent daily values based on the Reference Daily Intake (RDI) for a 2000 calorie diet.

Nutrition information calculated from recipe ingredients.

Amount Per Serving

Calories 299,07

Calories From Fat (56%) 166,02

% Daily Value

Total Fat 19,21g 30%

Saturated Fat 2,68g 13%

Cholesterol 75.52mg 25%

Hot Chicken and Avocado Nuts Salad (Instant Pot)

Ingredients

2 Tbsp Extra-virgin olive oil

3 cloves garlic

2 chicken breasts, chopped

4 ounces avocado (fresh diced)

1 stalk celery

1 bay leaf

1 cup beef broth

1 ground thyme

1 cup Macadamia Nuts

1/2 tsp cumin (toasted and ground)

Salt and ground pepper

3 Tbsp yellow mustard (without alcohol)

Instructions

1. Press SAUTÉ button on your Instant Pot
2. When the word "hot" appears on the display, add the oil and sauté the garlic about 3 - 4 minutes.
3. Add the chicken and sauté for 2 - 3 minutes; stir with wooden spoon.
4. Add all remaining ingredients (except mustard) and stir well.
5. Lock lid into place and set on the MANUAL setting for 10 minutes.
6. When the beep sounds, quick release the pressure by pressing Cancel, and twisting the steam handle to the Venting position.
7. Transfer salad to the serving plate and combine with the mustard.
8. Serve warm or cold.

Servings: 5

Cooking Times

Total Time: 20 minutes

Nutrition Facts

Serving size: 1/5 of a recipe (8 ounces)

Percent daily values based on the Reference Daily Intake (RDI) for a 2000 calorie diet.

Nutrition information calculated from recipe ingredients.

Amount Per Serving

Calories 128,07

Calories From Fat (77%) 98,12

% Daily Value

Total Fat 11,12g 17%

Saturated Fat 1,57g 8%

Cholesterol 0mg 0%

Sodium 45.13mg

Light Vegetable Soup (Instant Pot)

Ingredients

1/4 cup olive oil

2 leeks, sliced, white and light green

1/2 lb fresh spinach leaves

2 zucchini, finely sliced

2 medium potato, peeled and diced

2 3/4 cups water

A pinch of nutmeg

Salt and ground pepper to taste

Instructions

1. Press SAUTÉ button on your Instant Pot.
2. When the word "HOT" appears on the display, add

the oil and sauté about 5 minutes.

3. Add all remaining ingredients and stir well.
4. Lock lid into place and set on the MANUAL setting for 8 minutes.
5. Use Natural Release for 5 minutes and quick release remaining pressure.
6. Transfer soup in a blender and blend until soft. Serve.

Savory Salad Soup (Instant Pot)

Ingredients

2 Tbsp olive oil

1 large onion, finely diced

4 carrots, sliced

1 tomato, peeled and grated

1 stick of celery

1 bunch of parsley

4 large lettuce leaves, finely chopped

4 cups water

Salt and ground pepper to taste

Cayenne pepper

1/2 cup lemon juice

2 Tbsp fresh parsley, finely chopped

Instructions

1. Place all ingredients (except lemon juice) in your Instant Pot; stir well.
2. Lock lid into place and set on the MANUAL setting for 5 minutes.
3. When the beep sounds, quick release the pressure by pressing Cancel, and twisting the steam handle to the Venting position.
4. Transfer mixture to your fast-speed blender and blend until smooth.
5. Taste and adjust salt and pepper.
6. Sprinkle with lemon juice, and parsley; serve.

Nutrition Facts

Serving size: 1/4 of a recipe (5 ounces)

Percent daily values based on the Reference Daily Intake (RDI) for a 2000 calorie diet.

Nutrition information calculated from recipe ingredients.

Amount Per Serving

Calories 35,47

Calories From Fat (7%) 2,32

% Daily Value

Total Fat 0,28g <1%

Saturated Fat 0,06g <1%

Cholesterol 0mg 0%

Sodium 169.9mg

Steamed Asparagus Salad (Instant Pot)

Ingredients

1 bunch green asparagus (about 10 spears)

1 cup carrots, chopped

1 cup mushrooms, sliced

2 Tbsp lemon juice

Salt and ground pepper to taste

1 cup water for Instant Pot

Instructions

1. Cut the woody part of the asparagus and wash well.
2. Scrape the skin of carrots,

wash and cut into thin strips.

3. Wash the mushrooms and cut them into thin slices.
4. Pour the water and place the steamer basket into the Instant Pot.
5. Place your asparagus, carrots, and mushrooms onto the steamer basket.
6. Lock lid into place and set to Steaming and manually adjust it to 3 minutes
7. When the beep sounds, quick release the pressure by pressing Cancel, and twisting the steam handle to the Venting position.
8. Transfer vegetables to a plate.
9. Season the salt and pepper, pour the lemon juice, stir well and serve.

Servings: 4

Cooking Times

Total Time: 25 minutes

Nutrition Facts

Serving size: 1/4 of a recipe (6.5 ounces)

Percent daily values based on the Reference Daily Intake (RDI) for a 2000 calorie diet.

Nutrition information calculated from recipe ingredients.

Amount Per Serving

Calories 236,29

Calories From Fat (52%) 121,88

% Daily Value

Total Fat 13,8g 21%

Saturated Fat 1,93g 10%

Cholesterol 0mg 0%

Sweet Potato Wedges with Paprika (Instant Pot)

Ingredients

4 Tbsp olive oil

4 medium sweet potatoes, cut into wedges

1 -2 tsp smoked paprika

1 tsp cayenne pepper (more or less to taste)

1/2 cup water

Salt to taste

Instructions

1. Scrub the skin of sweet potatoes and slice in wedges.
2. Pour the oil and place the potatoes in your Instant Pot.
3. Add all remaining ingredients

and stir well.
4. Lock lid into place and set on the MANUAL setting for 15 minutes.
5. Use Natural Release for 10 minutes and quick release remaining pressure.
6. Taste and adjust seasonings to taste.
7. Serve hot.

Servings: 4

Cooking Times

Total Time: 20 minutes

Nutrition Facts

Serving size: 1/4 of a recipe (5.5 ounces)

Percent daily values based on the Reference Daily Intake (RDI) for a 2000 calorie diet.

Nutrition information calculated from recipe ingredients.

Amount Per Serving

Calories 106,11

Calories From Fat (57%) 60,05

% Daily Value

Total Fat 6,97g 11%

Saturated Fat 5,94g 30%

Cholesterol 0mg 0%

S N A C K S

"Baked" Butternut Squash Chips (Instant Pot)

Ingredients

1 lb butternut squash

2 Tbsp coconut oil (melted)

1 tsp ginger powder

1/4 tsp nutmeg

1 tsp cinnamon

1/8 tsp cloves

Pinch salt

1/2 cup water

Instructions

1. Clean and peel the butternut squash and slice.
2. Place the coconut oil in your Instant Pot and add the butternut squash.
3. Add all remaining ingredients and toss to combine well.
4. Lock lid into place and set on the MANUAL setting for 12 minutes.
5. When the timer beeps, press "Cancel" and carefully flip the Quick Release valve to let the pressure out.
6. Serve hot or keep refrigerated.

Nutrition Facts

Serving size: 1/6 of a recipe (8 ounces)

Percent daily values based on the Reference Daily Intake (RDI) for a 2000 calorie diet.

Nutrition information calculated from recipe ingredients.

Amount Per Serving

Calories 209,47

Calories From Fat (39%) 82,19

% Daily Value

Total Fat 9,32g 14%

Saturated Fat 1,31g 7%

Cholesterol 0mg 0%

Sodium 136.72mg

Aromatic Potato in Tomato Paste (Instant Pot)

Ingredients

4 Tbsp Olive oil

1 onion, chopped

1 clove garlic, finely chopped

4 large potatoes, cut into chunks

1 cup tomato paste (fresh or canned)

1 Tbsp Italian seasoning

1 cup water

Salt and pepper to taste

Instructions

1. Press SAUTÉ button on your

Instant Pot; when the display shows HOT, pour the oil.

2. Sauté the onion and garlic for 3 - 4 minutes or until soft.
3. Add the potatoes and sauté for 2 - 3 minutes.
4. Add all remaining ingredients and stir well.
5. Lock lid into place and set on the MANUAL setting for 5 minutes.
6. Use Quick Release - turn the valve from sealing to venting to release the pressure.
7. Mash the potatoes with the fork and stir well.
8. Serve hot.

Servings: 4

Cooking Times

Total Time: 15 minutes

Nutrition Facts

Serving size: 1/4 of a recipe (8 ounces)

Percent daily values based on the Reference Daily Intake (RDI) for a 2000 calorie diet.

Nutrition information calculated from recipe ingredients.

Amount Per Serving

Calories 199,04

Calories From Fat (62%) 122,73

% Daily Value

Total Fat 13,91g 21%

Saturated Fat 1,94g 10%

Cholesterol 0mg 0%

Carrots, Garlic and Lemon Salad (Instant Pot)

Ingredients

1/4 cup extra-virgin olive oil

2 onions, cut into rings

4 Tbsp mashed garlic cloves

6 medium carrots, shredded

1 Tbsp lemon juice

Instructions

1. Slice carrots and onions and season with salt.
2. Press SAUTÉ button on your Instant Pot.
3. When display show HOT pour the oil. Add onion and garlic and sauté for 2 - 3 minutes

until soft.

4. Add carrots and stir for two minutes.
5. Lock lid into place and set on the MANUAL setting for 2-3 minutes.
6. Use Natural Release for 10 minutes and quick release remaining pressure.
7. Pour the lemon juice over carrots and serve.

Servings: 4

Cooking Times

Total Time: 6 hours
and 5 minutes

Nutrition Facts

Serving size: 1/4 of
a recipe (5 ounces)

Percent   daily
values   based   on
the Reference Daily
Intake (RDI) for a
2000 calorie diet.

Nutrition
information
calculated   from
recipe ingredients.

Amount   Per
Serving

Calories 247,58

Calories From Fat
(72%) 178,35

% Daily Value

Total   Fat   19,8g
30%

Saturated Fat 6,44g
32%

Cholesterol 64,2mg
21%

Sodium   214.31mg

Hot Buffalo Chicken Wings (Instant Pot)

Ingredients

3 Tbsp lard or ghee

6 frozen chicken wings

1 cup cayenne peppers sauce

Salt to taste

Instructions

1. Add lard in your Instant Pot.
2. Place the chicken wings in Instant Pot and pour the hot sauce over chicken.
3. Season the chicken with the salt.
4. Lock lid into place and set on the MANUAL setting for 10 minutes.

5. Use Natural Release for 15 minutes and quick release remaining pressure.
6. Serve hot.

Servings: 4

Cooking Times

Total Time: 20 minutes

Nutrition Facts

Serving size: 1/4 of a recipe (7 ounces)

Percent daily values based on the Reference Daily Intake (RDI) for a 2000 calorie diet.

Nutrition information calculated from recipe ingredients.

Amount Per Serving

Calories 63,41

Calories From Fat (3%) 1,91

% Daily Value

Total Fat 0,23g <1%

Saturated Fat 0,05g <1%

Cholesterol 0mg 0%

Sodium 122.25mg

Instant Steamed Artichokes (Instant Pot)

Ingredients

4 whole artichokes

1 lemon wedge

1 cup water

Instructions

1. Rinse the artichokes with water; remove any damaged outer leaves. Using a knife, trim off the stem and top third of each artichoke.
2. Rub the cut top with a lemon wedge to prevent browning.
3. Pour a cup of water in your Instant Pot and place a steamer basket.

122

4. Place the artichokes on top of the steamer basket.
5. Close the lid in place and select "MANUAL" mode. Set the time for 8 minutes for medium artichokes.
6. Select Natural release in 10 minutes and then use a Quick release.
7. Serve warm artichokes with lemon.

Servings: 6

Cooking Times

Total Time: 10 minutes

Nutrition Facts

Serving size: 1/6 of a recipe (8 ounces)

Percent daily values based on the Reference Daily Intake (RDI) for a 2000 calorie diet.

Nutrition information calculated from recipe ingredients.

Amount Per Serving

Calories 91,85

Calories From Fat (47%) 42,97

% Daily Value

Total Fat 4,88g 8%

Saturated Fat 0,7g 4%

Cholesterol 0mg 0%

Sodium 78,78mg 3%

Light Mustard Cabbage (Instant Pot)

Ingredients

2 Tbsp extra-virgin olive oil

1 head green cabbage, chopped

2 carrots, shredded

1/2 tsp turmeric

1/2 tsp cumin

1 Tbsp of mustard

1 cup water

Sea salt and ground black pepper to taste

Instructions

1. Rinse, clean and chop the cabbage. Clean and shred the carrots.

2. Place all ingredients on the list in your Instant Pot.
3. Lock lid into place and set on the MANUAL setting LOW pressure for 3 minutes.
4. When the timer beeps, press "Cancel" and carefully flip the Quick Release valve to let the pressure out.
5. Serve warm.

Servings: 6

Cooking Times

Total Time: 15 minutes

Nutrition Facts

Serving size: 1/6 of a recipe (4 ounces)

Percent daily values based on the Reference Daily Intake (RDI) for a 2000 calorie diet.

Nutrition information calculated from recipe ingredients.

Amount Per Serving

Calories 106,68

Calories From Fat (39%) 42,07

% Daily Value

Total Fat 4,77g 7%

Saturated Fat 0,67g 3%

Cholesterol 0mg 0%

Sodium 106,06mg 4%

Parsnip Slices with Rosemary (Instant Pot)

Ingredients

2 parsnips, sliced

2 Tbsp extra-virgin olive oil

1 tsp rosemary finely chopped

Salt to taste

2 cups water

Instructions

1. Wash, peel and cut the parsnip into sticks.
2. Season the parsnip with the salt and rosemary.
3. Pour the oil over the parsnip and toss to combine well.
4. Pour 2 cups water into Instant Pot inner pot.

5. Place a steamer basket in inner pot.
6. Place the parsnip fingers on a steamer basket.
7. Lock lid into place and set on the MANUAL setting for 7 minutes.
8. Use Natural Release for 10 minutes and quick release remaining pressure.
9. Serve immediately.

Party Turkey Meatballs (Instant Pot)

Ingredients

3 Tbsp Extra-virgin olive oil

1 1/2 lbs ground turkey

6 slices turkey bacon

1/2 cup ground almond

Pinch of salt

1 egg

2 cloves garlic

1 tsp paprika

2 Tbsp tomato paste

Instructions

1. In a large bowl, add ground

turkey, turkey bacon, ground almonds, garlic and other spices; stir well.

2. Use your hands to shape meatballs with the turkey mixture.
3. Pour olive oil into your Instant Pot and place the meatballs.
4. Lock lid into place and set on the MANUAL setting for 10 minutes.
5. Use Quick Release - turn the valve from sealing to venting to release the pressure.
6. Serve hot.

Perfect Homemade Apple Sauce (Instant Pot)

Ingredients

12 medium apples, pilled and diced

1 cup apple juice, unsweetened (non-alcoholic)

1/2 tsp cinnamon

Instructions

1. Place the apples and apple juice in the inner pot of the Instant Pot.
2. Cover the lid and set the pressure valve to 'Sealing'
3. Press the button 'Manual' and adjust cooking time to 10 minutes.
4. When the timer beeps,

release the pressure naturally.
5. Transfer apple mixture to your blender and blend until smooth and creamy.
6. Keep refrigerated.

Maca Root Squash Chips (Instant Pot)

Ingredients

2 cups butternut squash

2 Tbsp extra virgin coconut oil, melted

1 1/2 tsp ginger, fresh, minced

1/4 tsp maca root powder (or nutmeg)

1 tsp cinnamon

1/8 tsp ground caraway seeds (or cumin)

Pinch of salt to taste

Instructions

1. Clean and peel the butternut squash, and slice with a mandoline slicer.
2. Place sliced butternut squash in a bowl and set aside.
3. In a separate bowl, mix melted coconut oil, ginger, maca, cinnamon, ground caraway seeds, and sweetener.
4. Pour the oil mixture over the butternut squash and toss well.
5. Add the coconut oil in your Instant Pot and place the butternut squash slices.
6. Lock lid into place and set on the MANUAL setting for 10 minutes.
7. Use Natural Release for 10 minutes and quick release remaining pressure.
8. Serve immediately.